ABC

ABC

An Alphabet Book

PHOTOGRAPHED IN COLOR
BY THOMAS MATTHIESEN

PLATT & MUNK, *Publishers* / NEW YORK

Published by Platt & Munk, 1968.
All rights reserved. Printed in Singapore.
Library of Congress Catalog Card No.:
66-13382
ISBN 0-8228-1050-6

A a

apple

Apples are a fruit and very good to eat.
The first bite of an apple tastes best,
but the last bite is fun, too.

B b

balloons

Balloons float in the air and bounce in the breeze. A balloon is a happy thing to have on the end of a string.

C c

clock

Clocks tell you what time it is when you get up in the morning and when you go to bed at night. You can learn to tell time by seeing where the hands are pointing.

D d

doll

Dolls can be either boys or girls, but they're
not real people. No one has ever seen
a doll grow up.

E e

eggs

Eggs have a white shell that protects the food inside them. It is not good to drop an egg unless you like to mop the floor.

F f

flowers

Flowers make the world look prettier.
They grow in every color and have names
just like people do. These white and yellow
ones are called daisies.

G g

guitar

A guitar makes wonderful sounds called music.
Wouldn't it be fun to play one?

H h

house

This house has rooms just like the rooms in your house. Which room do you like most, living room, bedroom, or kitchen?

I i

insect

Insects are usually tiny and crawl on the ground. But some can fly and they are the hardest to catch.

J j

jar

Jars hold lots of different things—
jam and flour, sugar and cereal.
Why is there a marble in this one?

K k

keys

Keys are used to open closed doors.
Have you ever seen a closed door and
wondered what was on the other side of it?

L l

lion

Lions usually live in the jungle far away.
But sometimes they live in zoos and that's
where you can see one. Never growl
at a lion. He will growl back.

M m

mittens

Mittens keep your hands warm when the weather is cold, and they are also very good for picking up snow.

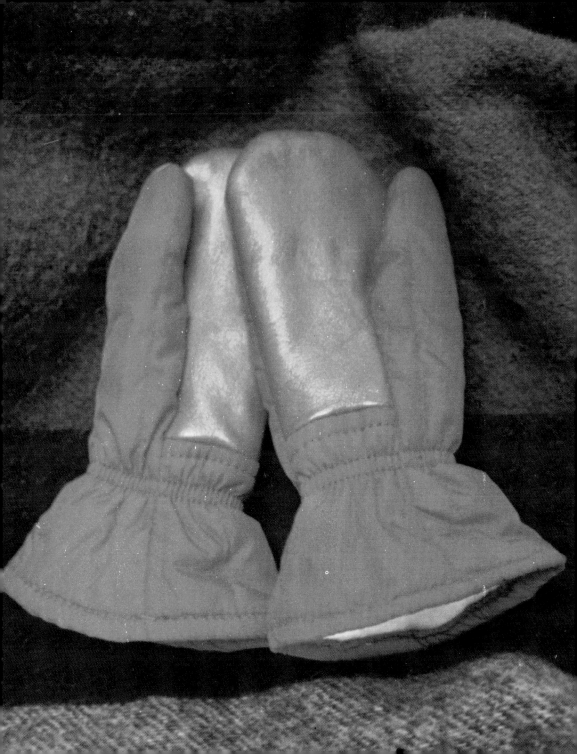

N n

newspaper

A newspaper is full of stories about what has happened to people all over the world. Can you read one?

O o

owl

An owl is a bird with large eyes.
Some people think owls are very smart.
No one knows if owls think people are smart.

P p
paint

Paint is many different colors. It can make a white room blue or a blue room yellow. How do you suppose it works?

Q q

quilt

Quilts are made of many different pieces of cloth sewn together, and when you get under one, it keeps you warm.

R r

rabbit

Rabbits like to sit in the grass and stare at things. But when people try to stare at them, they run away.

S s

shoes

Shoes keep your feet safe when you walk.
They have strings called laces,
which often become untied.

T t

telephone

A telephone lets you talk to people who are
very far away, even in other countries.
But you have to be able to understand
their language.

U u

umbrella

Umbrellas keep you dry when it rains.
They also keep the sun off your head
on the beach. This makes them very useful
things to have around.

V v

vase

Vases come in many shapes and sizes.

Usually they have flowers in them.

What color flowers would you put in this one?

W w

window

A window lets you see what is happening on the other side of it. Has anyone ever looked through a window in your house and seen you?

X x

xylophone

A xylophone is a musical instrument that you beat with tiny sticks. No matter how hard you hit it, a xylophone will never cry.

Y y

yarn

Yarn starts out as long strings, but when it is made into a sweater, it ends up as little knots. Don't you think that's strange?

Z z

zipper

A zipper has little teeth that bite together
and hold each other so tightly you can't
pull them apart—unless you know the secret.
Do you?

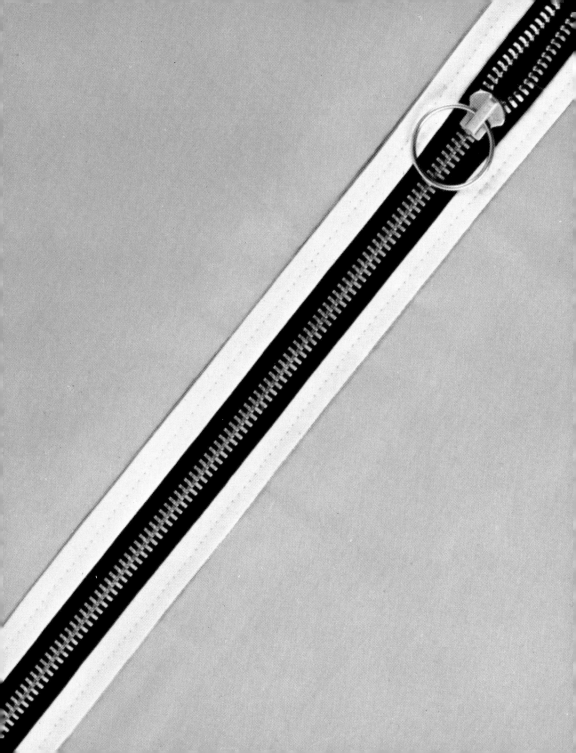

A B C